Vulnerability

The GOSPEL for REAL LIFE series

Abuse: Finding Hope in Christ
Anxiety: Anatomy and Cure
Borderline Personality: A Scriptural Perspective
Cutting: A Healing Response
God's Attributes: Rest for Life's Struggles
Vulnerability: Blessing in the Beatitudes

Brad Hambrick, Series Editor

Vulnerability

BLESSING IN THE BEATITUDES

BRAD HAMBRICK

PUBLISHING
P.O. BOX 817 • PHILLIPSBURG • NEW JERSEY 08865-0817

Printed in the United States of America

Library of Congress Cataloging-in-Publication Data

Hambrick, Brad, 1977-
  Vulnerability : blessing in the Beatitudes / Brad Hambrick.
    p. cm. -- (The Gospel for real life)
  ISBN 978-1-59638-416-3 (pbk.)
  1. Beatitudes--Criticism, interpretation, etc. 2. Risk taking (Psychology)--Religious aspects--Christianity. I. Title.
  BT382.H225 2012
  241.5'3--dc23
                                    2012006191

WHEN YOU HEAR the word *vulnerable*, you might think: "being in a defenseless position in the presence of a real threat that could do significant harm." If you are not quite that verbose, you might think: "being vulnerable means getting hurt." If that is how we think, then vulnerability is a bad thing, something to be avoided at all costs.

At first, that sounds good. I want to live a life without pain. Is that not what heaven will be, a place with no more pain (Rev. 21:4), a place where we cannot be hurt? Yes, to set your mind at ease, heaven is a place without pain or hurt. Yet it will be a place of complete vulnerability—we will be known completely, unable and not wanting to hide anything.

That last part might not sound so good. "Being known equals being hurt," we have learned to think. When people know you, that gives them the ability to influence or shame you. After all, "knowledge is power," right? Who has not experienced several of the following?

- A parent knows your past failures and brings them up during a lecture.
- A friend knows a secret and shares it, resulting in betrayal and embarrassment.
- A boss knows you cannot afford to leave your job and uses it as leverage to force extra work.
- A spouse knows your insecurities and uses them to win an argument.
- A child learns your past indiscretions and uses them as leverage when you try to discipline.
- A friend knows an embarrassing event and uses it as a public joke.

- A shameful event that no one knows makes it nearly impossible for you to receive love because "they do not know the real me."

That last one lets us see why vulnerability is good. Vulnerability is necessary in order to receive love. In the same way that oxygen is necessary for fire, I must let you know me before I can believe that you love me. Many people are excellent at loving, serving, giving, doing, achieving, and helping others. But their ability to receive love is severely muted by their unwillingness or seeming inability to be vulnerable. This can look like any of the following:

- A very academic approach to your faith, because understanding the facts is "safer" than depending on your beliefs.
- Relationships in which you do more for and know more about other people than they do for or know about you.
- A high drive for achievement and fairness, because you want to be sure to earn what you get and be in "debt" (relationally or emotionally) to no one.
- A distrust or dislike of emotions, because they allow others to see too much of you and you are less in control when you experience them.
- A belief that others "know the unwritten rules of relationships" that no one has told you, and a resulting fear or resentment of relationships.
- A discomfort with just being with another person that results in your relationships' disproportionately depending on activities to keep them going.
- An enduring urge to "make things right" after a conflict or sin that keeps the fault at the center of your relationships and your thoughts for a long time.

These things prevent us from receiving love. Usually they produce an imbalance in relationships that results in our feeling "used." But when our lack of vulnerability does not allow us to be loved, our relationships will always end in our feeling used. For us to resent others for a situation that was brought on by our own approach to a relationship is contradictory.

By this point you may be thinking, "I am not sure what you are talking about when you say *vulnerable*. I do not see how 'letting people hurt me' is going to result in anything good. So what if I do those things you listed? That is still better than being hurt." We can begin to address those concerns by defining our key term:

> *Vulnerability* is the willingness to take the risk of allowing any event, belief, preference, interest, or emotion of your life to be "on the table" when it is useful to glorify God by encouraging a fellow believer, allowing a fellow believer to encourage you, or evangelizing an unbeliever. It is this disposition that breathes the life of authenticity into relationships and allows them to be mutually enjoyable, enriching, and character-shaping.

Five aspects of this definition are worth exploring.

First, vulnerability requires only the *willingness* to share and should not be confused with the constant obligation to share. A healthy vulnerability is not the same as "vomiting" one's life on every available listener. It simply removes "my protection" as the reason for nondisclosure before the conversation begins. The protective balance to this will be given in the fifth aspect.

Second, vulnerability does involve *risk*. No amount of rightly applied wisdom will completely remove the risk involved in making yourself known to another person. Once you give information to another person, you are no longer exclusively in control of what is done with that information. An important question to ask yourself is: "When I resist being vulnerable, what am I unwilling to risk?"

Third, vulnerability does involve the *full breadth of human experience*. To the degree that we hold back parts of our person from someone, we will limit our ability to be or feel loved by that person. Not every relationship is meant to connect at every level of human experience. But the limits should be determined by the nature of the relationship, not our fear.

Fourth, vulnerability is *purposeful*. Like everything else in life, vulnerability is healthy only when it is engaged in for the glory of God. As a relational interaction, vulnerability glorifies God by allowing a believer (you or the other person) to be encouraged or by serving as a bridge to a gospel conversation with an unbeliever (usually by revealing some aspect of your need for Christ).

Fifth, vulnerability should be a *mutual* activity. If vulnerability is one-sided, it becomes unhealthy. Vulnerability is a quality that is grown into. If you are disclosing more than the other person is reciprocating, then you are likely either unduly elevating your expectation of the relationship or trying to accelerate the other person's growth in vulnerability. This inevitably results in people's getting hurt and vulnerability's getting a bad name.

The question now becomes: "Where do we find instruction for growing in this kind of vulnerability?" We can look in a concordance and not get much help. Even the most modern translations and paraphrases lack the word *vulnerability*. But I have found one portion of Scripture to be saturated with descriptions of vulnerability—the Beatitudes in Matthew 5:3–11. Take a moment and read through these verses. Let the fact that Jesus declares each description good ("blessed") resonate with you. Notice how each boldface phrase is a description of the kind of vulnerability that we have been talking about.

> *Blessed* are **the poor in spirit**, for theirs is the kingdom of heaven.
> *Blessed* are **those who mourn**, for they shall be comforted.
> *Blessed* are **the meek**, for they shall inherit the earth.
> *Blessed* are **those who hunger and thirst** for righteousness, for they shall be satisfied.
> *Blessed* are **the merciful**, for they shall receive mercy.

Blessed are **the pure in heart**, for they shall see God.

Blessed are **the peacemakers**, for they shall be called sons of God.

Blessed are **those who are persecuted** for righteousness' sake, for theirs is the kingdom of heaven.

Blessed are you when others **revile you and persecute you** and utter all kinds of evil against you falsely on my account. (Matt. 5:3–11)

It is significant that these declarations come at the beginning of the Sermon on the Mount (Matt. 5–7). Jesus was using them to prepare his listeners to understand and apply the longest continuous discourse we have from Christ—one rich with teaching on the emotional and relational life of his followers.

Notice the subjects that follow the Beatitudes. The commentary afterward tries to capture the fears or cynicism that would emerge as a response to the rest of the Sermon on the Mount if we had an errant or incomplete view of vulnerability. Not all the struggles may fit you, but mark the ones that do. It will help you with the reflective sections in the devotional portions of this booklet.

- *Willingness to exert influence in relationships* (Matt. 5:13–16): If I speak up about who I am, what I believe, or what I like, then people could reject me or use those things against me.
- *Relating to rules and expectations* (5:17–20): I wish Christ had come to follow the Law instead of to fulfill it. Learning to love God completely and loving others is much more risky than following protocols.
- *Anger* (5:21–26): Jesus took my defense. It is safer to be angry than hurt. Now when I lash out, I am not protecting my heart—I am jeopardizing my soul.
- *Lust or counterfeit intimacy* (5:27–30): Relationships are safer in my imagination. I can get what I want without risking rejection.

- *Divorce or broken relationships* (5:31–32): I want to reserve the right to end a relationship on my terms. If I am not happy, then I should be free to end a relationship.
- *Broken promises* (5:33–37): I do not like it when other people have expectations of me. It creates pressure. I feel measured. I wish everyone said what they meant.
- *Desire for revenge* (5:38–42): But they hurt me first. Am I supposed to keep letting myself be hurt? When do I get to have a say?
- *Longing for equity and love* (5:43–48): It's not enough that I cannot get even; now I have to love my enemy. I want to make justice happen in order to be safe.
- *Responding to the needs of others* (6:1–4): I do not mind helping others so much, but it always becomes unhealthy. I am always the one in the role of helper and never the one seen to be in need, even when I am in need.
- *Doing things for the approval of others* (6:5–18): How else am I supposed to get the approval of others? I thought doing good things so that people would like you was a good thing. That is another "safe" way of relating to people that Jesus is taking away from me.
- *Finances and priorities* (6:19–24): Money is something else that allows me not to be vulnerable. As long as I have enough money, I do not have to depend on anyone else. It means that people come to me, instead of my going to them.
- *Anxiety* (6:25–34): Great—I feel anxious frequently, and that is wrong, too. I am supposed to be real with people, rely on people, and enjoy it.
- *Conflict resolution* (7:1–6): I hate conflict. I hate being judge. I do not trust people to take the speck out of their eye when I take the log out of mine.
- *Expectations of a father* (7:7–11): What if my father did give me a stone and a serpent? Where do you think I learned that trust was a bad idea?

- *Treatment of others* (7:12–14): The hard part is often letting others do for me as I am willing to do for them. When I let others do for me, they could disappoint or hurt me.
- *Discerning liars* (7:15–20): By the time I see their fruit, it is too late to prevent being hurt. If the point is to avoid being hurt, Jesus' test does not help me very much.
- *The ineffective effort of "earning" acceptance* (7:21–23): I could do lots of stuff for God and he might still turn his back on me? What is it that God wants if it is not for me to serve him?
- *The necessity of putting what you learn into practice* (7:24–27): Allow me to encourage you. In light of whatever doubt or fear you feel, building on the "rock" of Jesus' teaching is the place to start and worth the effort.

Until we see the "blessedness" of the Beatitudes, we will wrestle with these questions and doubts, distort or miss the application of these passages, and still be unable to receive the love of God and others. Once we see the blessedness and begin to grow in the courageous application of the Beatitudes, the wisdom and joy of Jesus' teaching will begin to shine in and through our lives by yielding the fruits of hope and peace, attractive witness to and love for others.

From this point forward, we will begin to examine each of the Beatitudes. I recommend initially reading straight through the material as you would an article. Then I advise coming back and studying each beatitude devotionally, taking time to consider the personal reflection and prayer sections.

Each beatitude will have five points of examination:

1. *Description*: Definition of the disposition, role, or activity that Jesus says is "blessed."
2. *Benefit for Vulnerability*: The connection between that beatitude and a healthy sense or acceptance of vulnerability.
3. *Implementation*: Possible ways that you could begin the process of growing in this facet of vulnerability.

4. *Personal Reflection*: Questions to assist you in examining your life in light of the particular beatitude. When you go back through and read these materials devotionally, you may want to record your reflections in a notebook or journal.

5. *Prayer*: A sample guided prayer to help you to bring this area of growth before the Lord regularly. Remember, we never grow apart from the grace of God empowering us, and prayer is the initial and primary way in which we demonstrate our dependence on and vulnerability toward God. These sample prayers are intended to be made your own.

Under each beatitude you will see "□ Yes □ No ___/10 Intensity ___ /8 Rank." The "Yes" and "No" boxes are a place for you to mark whether you understood the material under that beatitude. Chances are, if vulnerability is a significant struggle for you, then certain sections will be counterintuitive enough for you that they may be hard to understand or accept. Be patient, knowing that you may need to spend extra time on that beatitude when you go back through the material devotionally.

The 1-to-10 scale is a place for you to rank the intensity of your struggle with that aspect of vulnerability. Ideally, you will be encouraged to find several aspects of vulnerability that come more naturally to you. Identifying the various degrees of struggle should help you to develop a plan of application at the end of the booklet.

The 1-to-8 scale is a place for you to rank the Beatitudes from the personally hardest to easiest, to express aspects of vulnerability. This scale is to be filled in only after you have completed the entire booklet. The goal of these rankings is to help you to see that *vulnerability* is not one giant, monolithic term. It can be broken down into related, bite-size pieces that you can strategically work on (by God's grace) in the ways that seem wisest and best fit your life.

"POOR IN SPIRIT"

□ Yes □ No ___ /10 Intensity ___ /8 Rank

Description: Simply stated, to be poor in spirit means to realize and accept that life requires more than I have to give. Yet it is more akin to humility than desperation or pessimism. Those who have traveled outside America realize that the truly poor are some of the world's most generous people. Life is bigger than they are, but that does not impede their joy, love, work, or service. To be poor in spirit is to realize that those things I have were given to me to bless others (Gen. 12:1–3) and that therefore I am poor. An analogy might be drawn to a man driving an armored car. He is literally loaded with cash, but the money is neither his nor for him.

The blessings of life (grace, love, money, pleasure, talent, charisma, relationships) are intended to glorify God. Our joy should be in dispensing these blessings, not hoarding them. Those who are poor in spirit do not take ownership of life's blessings and therefore become defensive, prideful, or protective. Rather, they view themselves as a conduit of these blessings, looking to multiply the blessings through sharing them.

Benefit for Vulnerability: Being poor in spirit removes the fear of "being found out" or revealed as inadequate. This fear undergirds many struggles with vulnerability. Being poor in spirit allows me to walk into a room and not compare myself to the others in the room. The one who is poor in spirit is not competing or seeking to be recognized. The goal of achieving greatness or being special is replaced with the goals of faithfulness and contentment. The audience to which they play has been significantly shrunk (ideally down to One). If we are concerned with what *they* (plural) think, we are missing the point of being poor in spirit.

This is different from being callous or indifferent toward people (that disposition is soured by bitterness and cynicism).

Being poor in spirit allows us to be vulnerable by simply rec-
ognizing that we are (at our best) simply a conduit of God's
blessings and that we are not a special blessing ourselves (with
all the pressures that such a role would bring). We are free to
love without having to measure up, because the gift is not us.

Implementation: Is this really blessed? With all the Beatitudes, we will be challenged by this question if we take them
seriously. In order to agree with Jesus about the blessedness of
being poor in spirit, we must wrestle with this question: "What
really matters?" Take a look at the areas in which you struggle
to be vulnerable (real, authentic, free, relaxed) and ask yourself:
"What does this struggle reveal to be most important?" Is it
status, image, competence, athleticism, intelligence, or achievement? What kind of "rich" are you after? When you identify
each variable, repent of allowing it to be your measure of rich-
ness. That place is reserved for Christ's presence in our heart
and being an instrument of his (2 Cor. 8:9).

Resist the opposite temptation to use this beatitude as a reason
to refuse all compliments or consistently talk negatively about
yourself. When someone compliments you, rejoice with the person
about what God has done in his or her life through you. Like a
good impoverished host, celebrate the moment, relationship, or
blessing more than focusing on the scrawny chicken in the soup.

Personal Reflection: What aspects of the description of being
poor in spirit challenge you most? What remaining questions
do you have regarding how being poor in spirit equips you to be
wisely vulnerable? What changes do you need to make in order
to become more poor in spirit?

Who exemplifies the "rich" that you are after? What other
fears or insecurities does being poor in spirit stir within you?
How does this beatitude help you to think differently about
applying Philippians 2:1–11? Is the humble Jesus your hero?

What kind of freedom would you experience if you surrendered your "rich" to God?

Prayer: Lord, I do not want to daily depend on you for [list]. I am so easily fooled into believing that life would be better if I were not reliant on you for those things. I fear you in an unhealthy way; I am trying to rely on you less, not more. The thought of surrendering my life [list dreams] so that I can gain life is awkward to me (Luke 9:23–24). I want a guarantee, but I know that beggars (the poor in spirit) cannot be choosers. I want to be special in myself, but I know my happiness is found in you. Yet I know the very things that I am begging you for are the things that keep me up at night. I would sleep better and laugh more often if you replaced them in my heart. Father, grant me the courage to love with empty, open hands. Help me to see that being poor in spirit means that I have nothing to lose and that being "rich in my own eyes" means that I must protect everything. Teach me to be generous with my very self (possessions, story, emotions, and talents) for your glory and the benefit of others.

"THOSE WHO MOURN"

☐ Yes ☐ No ___/10 Intensity ___/8 Rank

Description: Mourning is the painful recognition that something treasured is absent. Because one's treasure is obvious to others during mourning, the experience of mourning is often confused as *weakness* (a negative synonym for *vulnerability*; see "The Meek" below). The logic is: "If people can see what I miss, they might think it's silly, believe I'm overreacting, use it against me, or judge me for it." Those who mourn are evidencing that they believe their treasured person, object, activity, or identity is worth the risk.

Mourning is often avoided or viewed negatively because it is unpleasant. A predominant value of our culture is that only things that are pleasant are good, that all things unpleasant are bad (suffering has no value). This false belief causes shame or awkwardness whenever we are not happy. We often live as though the command to "rejoice in the Lord always" (Phil. 4:4) made the command to "weep with those who weep" (Rom. 12:15) wrong. We miss the connection that mourning is celebrating through tears the goodness of some blessing now painfully absent. Therefore, we fail to invite others into that experience, especially if we view the grief as small (inadvertently "weighing" God's blessings). Because of this privatization of our mourning, we usually see others at their best, and this false belief is further reinforced.

Benefit for Vulnerability: It is hard to be vulnerable if only happiness is acceptable and my treasure (those things that give me peace, security, hope, or identity) can be known by only a select inner circle on the occasion of "major" losses. Romans 12:15–16 says, "Rejoice with those who rejoice, weep with those who weep. Live in harmony with one another. Do not be haughty, but associate with the lowly." Here we have a biblical command that necessitates the sharing of both pleasant and unpleasant emotions. Therefore, to resist being vulnerable is to live contrary to God's design for our lives (and will carry the negative consequences of any other disobedience to God).

Allowing our treasure to be known is also a part of the Christian life. Matthew 6:21 says, "For where your treasure is, there your heart will be also." Part of our being salt and light to the world around us (Matt. 5:13–14) is the living testimony of the functionality of our treasure and the freedom we have in Christ to mourn its absence. If we, as Christians, are guarded with our treasure, then either (1) we have focused our life on the wrong treasure and we are muted by our guilt or embarrassment or (2) we have a wrong view of what we are to do with our treasure and how all our emotions are meant to give public, compelling testimony to the things that are really important in life.

Implementation: First, you must discern whether your resistance to mourning is a result of shame (mourning is unacceptable) or fear (mourning reveals me, and I prefer to remain hidden). If the resistance emerges from shame, then you need to either allow your beliefs regarding unpleasant emotions to be challenged by the God who cares enough to keep your every tear in a bottle (Ps. 56:8) or evaluate the healthiness of your circle of relationships (past and present) and their influence on your practice of emotions.

If the resistance emerges from fear, then you need to evaluate whether your treasure has become something less permanent and stable than God, or whether you have constructed some set of rules or protocols by which you believe you must ensure the safety of your treasure. As dependent creatures, we have had our lives designed by God so that our Ultimate Treasure should protect us, instead of our trying to protect our treasure. This is the definition of peace and freedom that enables healthy vulnerability.

Make a list of the things that are no longer a part of your life and that make you sad to be without (people, activities, groups, season of life, and so on). Beside each one, write what was good about that blessing. Describe the positive influence that each one had on your life and the lessons you learned or memories you treasure. If nostalgia or sadness emerges, recognize the emotion as a way of celebrating these past blessings. Look for an opportunity to share one of these memories or lessons in the coming days.

Personal Reflection: What aspects of the description of mourning challenge you most? What remaining questions do you have regarding how mourning equips you to be wisely vulnerable? What changes do you need to make in order to become free to mourn?

Why have you been tempted to hide your mourning or other unpleasant emotional expressions (personal beliefs or relational experiences)? What is the most attractive expression of grief that you can remember seeing in someone else? How would the freedom to mourn in the presence of others enable you to receive love and be more authentic in relationships?

Prayer: Lord, I do not like being sad. It makes me and those around me uncomfortable. I have a hard time imagining that you would want to be near me at those times (Pss. 34:18; 147:3; Isa. 61:1). I feel like a wounded animal—unsafe—when I am sad around others. I need you to change the way I think. I am not trying to be defiant when I hide. I have been trying to shield others. Father, please bring people into my life that I can be honest and open with. Give me the opportunity to see someone mourn in a healthy way. When I see it, make the healthiness of that person's unpleasant emotional expression attractive to me. I do not want to always have to be strong and self-protecting. Free me from the bondage of my own fears.

"THE MEEK"

☐ Yes ☐ No ___ /10 Intensity ___ /8 Rank

Description: The most common and very accurate definition of *meekness* is "power under control." The tendency of fallen humanity is to emphasize one or the other. Either we are powerful (confident and open to the point of arrogance, foolishness, or blindness) or we are under control (withdrawn, suspicious, or measured to the point that relationships are fake, optional, superficial, or dissatisfying). Meekness is that balance of a firm, principled sense of identity with the calm, open-minded awareness of personal weaknesses, others, and situational challenges.

Benefit for Vulnerability: Vulnerability requires both confidence and restraint. Meekness jettisons the all-or-nothing disposition of guardedness. Without the concept of meekness, vulnerability feels like a chasm to leap ("I have to get there") rather than a balance to walk ("I am avoiding two opposite extreme reactions").

Meekness makes vulnerability as much about character as it is about skill. Vulnerability is less about conversational ability (although that can play a part) than it is about a balanced set of goals and expectations in a relationship. Too often in the struggle to be vulnerable, our focus immediately jumps to how we are interacting with people instead of seeing how our perspective on "who we are" and "what relationships are about" dictates our interactions. Meekness forces us to examine our sense of identity and what we want from relationships before we try to learn new ways to talk or relate to people.

Implementation: Recognize when you are likely to struggle with overemphasizing power or control. Both are likely to be present—one primary and the other a compensation for our more natural overemphasis (I am quiet and don't address concerns until I become overwhelmed and blow up). Note the circumstances, types of relationships, or personal values that trigger the compensation. In terms of meekness and vulnerability, these triggers typically have something to do with safety. Completing the sentence "I feel safe only when _____ is true" should help to lead you to the answer.

A failure to be meek most often reveals a sense of safety that is rooted in something other than God's care and provision. Tracing our guardedness back to our relationship with God helps us to identify what aspect of God's character or redemption we need to grow in our understanding of or reliance on.

Personal Reflection: What aspects of the description of being meek challenge you most? What remaining questions do you have regarding how being meek equips you to be wisely vulnerable? What changes do you need to make in order to become more meek?

What social skills do you think you need to learn before you can be more vulnerable? What kind of person (character, beliefs, identity) expresses those skills? Do you know someone who expresses that character? How would pursuing that type of character be more effective than trying to master certain skills?

Prayer: Lord, I know I naturally lean toward [power or control], and this prevents me from enjoying relationships or blessing others as you intended. I tend to do this by [list patterns of behavior]. These habits have been my refuge for a long time. They are like old friends that I know I can count on. If I am going to "break up" with those patterns, I am going to have to really be able to count on you. I know you are dependable (Deut. 4:31; Josh. 1:5; John 14:18; Heb. 13:5); I just needed to admit how hard this is going to be. When I feel weak and want to return to my "friends," remind me quickly that I am never safe apart from active reliance on you. Settle in my heart that I am not clever, strong, or skilled enough to be safe except when I live as you prescribe.

"THOSE WHO HUNGER AND THIRST"

☐ Yes ☐ No ___ /10 Intensity ___ /8 Rank

Description: To hunger and thirst is to admit our dependence. To hunger and thirst for righteousness is to admit that we do not have a suitable righteousness of our own. Simply put, we are not good enough. Too often we are like the macho teenage boy in short sleeves on a winter day saying, "I'm not cold," while trying not to shiver. Biblically, life is not about a high self-esteem. Life is about confident reliance on God's sufficiency and surrendering our inadequacies to his grace.

The emphasis of this verse is not on the reality of lacking (shame), but on admitting to that lacking (dependence). The great paradox of this beatitude is that by admitting our deficiency, we receive the grace necessary to overcome it. If we are too prideful or insecure (two sides of the same coin) to openly acknowledge our deficiency, we will go through life with an insatiable hunger and no way to stop the cravings. The result is increasingly broken lives as we try to satisfy the hunger with everything but active, open reliance on God.

Benefit for Vulnerability: Vulnerability requires silencing the fear of being found out. Creating ever more elaborate disguises does not work. Even the greatest secret agents begin to doubt their disguises when they are in a den of thieves. Acknowledging our hunger (deficiency, weakness, or insecurity) allows us to live in the real world, as opposed to the fabricated world where we have to portray that we have it all together.

This is not the exhibitionistic telling of all our problems to everyone. Rather, it is placing all our inadequacies, hurts, and sins in the hands of God to allow them to be used at his discretion for the advancement of his kingdom by encouraging, instructing, or identifying with his other hurting people. This hunger (acknowledging dependence) is a hunger for righteousness because it longs for God to redeem every aspect of our lives (even the unappealing) for his glory.

Implementation: Reflect on the parable of the talents (Matt. 25:14–30). What are the one-talent equivalents of your life—those things that you want to bury and hide for fear of God's or other people's scorn? Make a list of events, physical attributes, abilities, or embarrassments. Before doing anything else, bring those to God in prayer and make them "available" for whenever or however he might use them for his glory.

Then pray that God would reveal to you an opportunity to use an item on your list to encourage, instruct, or identify with someone else. Study for a biblical perspective on each item on your list so that when the moment comes, your attitude, words, and actions will reflect God's heart. Pray that when the moment comes, God will give you both the courage to speak and the heart to rejoice in the opportunity. Pray that God will eventually give you the ability to rejoice in and give thanks for those aspects of your life that you currently do not want to acknowledge (2 Cor. 12:7–10).

Personal Reflection: What aspects of the description of being hungry and thirsty challenge you most? What remaining questions do you have regarding how being hungry and thirsty equips you to be wisely vulnerable? What changes do you need to make in order to become more hungry and thirsty?

How have you defined *bad* in ways other than "not useful for God's purposes"? How have you defined *good* in ways other than "useful for God's purposes"? How would embracing these definitions of *good* and *bad* free you to risk engaging in relationships more fully?

Prayer: Lord, there are many parts of my life that I thought I had to hide from you and others. Because I did not reveal them to you (in confession or for comfort), I realize that I could never reveal them to anyone else (to minister or receive comfort). Help me to desire usefulness to you more than I fear rejection or ridicule. Let my strongest craving be to model more of your character and see your redemption penetrate the most private areas of my life. It scares me to pray that, so I guess that is where we need to start. Thank you for letting me start with just you. Your patient, tender care motivates me (stirs my appetite) to go further in spite of my fear.

"THE MERCIFUL"

□ Yes □ No ___ /10 Intensity ___ /8 Rank

Description: Mercy is not fair. Those who are merciful necessarily come up on the short end of the stick at times. If I am going to be merciful, I must be willing to lose; something must be more important to me than losing. That is the gritty side of mercy that we all naturally resist. That is the side of mercy that makes many who try to practice it doormats. Actual mercy is not being a doormat, but it is in that direction.

Mercy is the willingness to accept personal loss for the good of another for a worthwhile cause. Often it is the neglect of that final clause ("for a worthwhile cause") that weakens our attempts to be merciful. The worthwhile cause for Christian mercy is the fame and declaration of God's character. Mercy says, "If God is glorified, I am willing to surrender what I am due from someone who has sinned against me or lived foolishly." Mercy forgives without condoning or overlooking the sin or folly. Mercy acknowledges sin and folly for what they are, but bears consequences that it does not owe in order to make God's character known and loved.

Benefit for Vulnerability: It is impossible to be vulnerable while insisting on winning or complete fairness. Those who are competitive or meticulous rule-followers will struggle with this aspect of vulnerability. In a fallen world, where redemption exists, truth and justice will not always "win" in the way that we think of winning.

The key to wise vulnerability is both the willingness to sacrifice and the ability to discern when the worthwhile cause of God's glory can (and cannot) be advanced by forgiving. Labeling every offense an opportunity to display God's grace (alleviation of consequences) is well-intentioned naiveté. Mercy is the balance of grace and truth in relationships. Mercy is wise and discerning about when to go the extra mile and when consequence is the best and appropriate means of God's grace (Heb. 12:1–13). Mercy is willing to call a Pharisee a "whitewashed tomb" (Matt. 23:27) but also willing to allow a prostitute to "go, and from now on sin no more" (John 8:11). When we are willing to personally lose for a cause greater than ourselves, wise vulnerability is possible.

Implementation: Wise mercy will not be practiced in isolation. This is partly because mercy requires an offending party. But more than that, we must acknowledge that none of us contains the wisdom and discernment necessary to consistently dispense balanced mercy. Mercy requires the involvement, perspective, and accountability of the body of Christ. Denial, harshness, pet peeves, idealizing, and glossing over will taint our individualistic attempts to be merciful. We need one another in order to properly reflect God's character.

Mercy requires allowing your judgment to be questioned. Therefore, mercy requires not only the risk of being wronged, but also the risk of admitting that you might be wrong. This means that you must begin with someone, preferably two to three people, and open your evaluations and perspective to critique: "Did I overreact to this situation? Was my response of hurt proportionate to that offense? Did I read a wrong meaning into what was said to me? Were my expectations too high?" Implementing mercy for the purpose of becoming vulnerable requires an initial investment of vulnerability. Choose wisely and persevere with that person or those people.

Personal Reflection: What aspects of the description of being merciful challenge you most? What remaining questions do you have regarding how being merciful equips you to be wisely vulnerable? What changes do you need to make in order to become more merciful?

When or how has foolish mercy caused you to shy away from mercy? What should you learn from those events (and not that mercy is bad)? Who is the most attractive example of "wise mercy" that you can think of?

Prayer: Lord, mercy confuses me. Because it does not follow a strict set of rules, I am not sure what to do with it. You know my bad experiences that have arisen from my trying to be merciful [list]. I just do not want to be hurt again. I do not have the wisdom to be good at mercy, so I am going to really need you for this one (James 1:5). I have never understood how you did what you did on the cross and were not the loser, but you did not lose. I guess that is why I cannot see how I can be merciful and not be the loser. Grant me the courage to be vulnerable through mercy so that I can better appreciate and model your great work on the cross.

"THE PURE IN HEART"

□ Yes □ No ___/10 Intensity ___/8 Rank

Description: The pure in heart do not choose expediency over rightness. The pure in heart do not fudge because "it's just easier that way." The pure in heart have chosen certain convictions that will govern their lives, and they do not depart from them. These convictions emerge from and are the relational, emotional, volitional expressions of the priorities of Scripture.

Being a person of conviction is essential to being biblically vulnerable. Great plots (and comic books) are written as the convictions of the superhero are used against him (superpowers do not remove the vulnerability of virtue)—he can either save the train full of people or catch the villain. The villain gets away, but integrity is maintained. The hero was manipulated. His virtue was used against him. Evil lived to fight another day. But the hero remains a hero: a person of character and integrity who is admired and can be emulated.

Benefit for Vulnerability: Without purity of heart (loving convictions), vulnerability is sidestepped for personal gain, ease, revenge, or self-protection. Vulnerability requires principles. A person who stands for nothing (or little of substance) is a moving target or someone who is not relevant enough to be targeted. One of the common themes of significant figures in church history is that they took stands for truth and were often scorned (or worse) for it. Purity of heart—knowing what is important in life and sacrificing for the goodness of those things—is a foundational element of vulnerability.

If someone does not take a genuine stand, the only opposition that he or she will face is perceived opposition. Vulnerability will be a battle of that person's imagination. This does not mean that it is easier. Battles of imagination are often harder to fight because the opponent has no physical body and is ever present in the creative mind of the afflicted. Being pure in heart makes vulnerability count for something (imaginary vulnerability is meaningless), and this serves as positive motivation for humble perseverance in the face of opposition.

Implementation: Decide what is worth being vulnerable for. What are the convictions, principles, and relationships for which you are willing to suffer (physically, emotionally, relationally, or financially)? A man without a cause can die on a thousand hills and will run from every elevation on his path. Vulnerability is confusing, meaningless, and wasteful unless there is a worthwhile cause. This helps to answer the question: "Must I just tell everyone everything about myself? Do I become an emotionally exhibitionistic person?" No; vulnerability should serve a purpose.

Vulnerability is the expression of a pure heart that is committed to the glory of God, the advancement of God's kingdom, the truth of Scripture, and the good of one's fellow man. When my social risk advances these things, I commit to keeping my heart true to my (God's) convictions. For example, husbands love their wives (vulnerable) as a public portrait of the gospel; or we are honest about our sins and shortcomings (vulnerable), bearing testimony that it is the truth met with grace that brings freedom, not hiding (John 8:31–38). Ultimately, we will seek to display the full spectrum of our emotions in order to accurately reflect the complete image of God to a world that has many misperceptions of God's character and purpose.

Personal Reflection: What aspects of the description of being pure in heart challenge you most? What remaining questions do you have regarding how being pure in heart equips you to be wisely vulnerable? What changes do you need to make in order to become more pure in heart?

When have you had being pure in heart used against you? Does it intimidate you to know that people might predict how you will respond? How do consistency and integrity create an atmosphere for healthier relationships?

Prayer: Lord, being pure in heart should sound better to me than it does, but it feels as though I am giving the world a competitive advantage over me. I prefer to keep my options open. Purity does not feel free. But I guess I would not be reading this booklet if I were really as free as I thought. Help me to see that guilt and shame are the real bondage, while grace and integrity are true freedom. God, you know that I need "eyes to see" that truth (Ezek. 12:2). I agree with you that "as the heavens are higher than the earth, so are my ways higher than your ways and my thoughts than your thoughts" (Isa. 55:9). Lord, meet me where I am, and give me the courage to walk toward you.

"THE PEACEMAKERS"

□ Yes □ No ___ /10 Intensity ___ /8 Rank

Description: Peacemakers are able to hold the convictions of the pure in heart without attacking those who disagree with them. Vulnerability is the balance of all eight attributes, not emphasizing any two or three of them over the rest. Peacemakers do not compromise, yet they do not lose sight of the people who need to be reached with the truth to which they cling.

Peacemakers do not retreat from conflict in fear. Conflict is the very context in which they are called to be peacemakers. If we are called to be the light of the world, we must expect to have to shine in darkness (Matt. 5:14). Peacemakers are able to recognize that disagreements are not ultimately about them.

Issues do not become personal and thereby inflame the emotional vigor of the conversation.

Benefit for Vulnerability: Vulnerability requires facing conflict and being able to maintain a focus on the issue or issues at hand. Recognize that being a peacemaker requires being in awkward, tense conversations. This is where a Christian belongs. Often those who struggle to be vulnerable feel as though they are doing something wrong if they are in such awkward or contentious conversations. While you as a Christian should not be contentious (2 Tim. 2:24–25), you can rest in the fact that the call to be a peacemaker frees you from this guilt.

When I realize that conflict is not about me, even when I am part of the subject, this also frees me. In James 4:1–6, the believers who were fighting were not confronted about being unfaithful to one another, but to God. When someone is rude, harsh, or mean, that person is primarily breaking the first Great Commandment of Matthew 22:37–39, not the second. When we overpersonalize the offense, we are emotionally reversing the priority of the offense. Like Moses when he angrily struck the rock and scolded the children of Israel, we are wrong for not maintaining the focus on God's holiness (Num. 20:1–13). We erroneously lead the other person to believe (because we believe it at that moment) that his or her *primary* offense is against us rather than God.

Implementation: Resist the temptation to think that an awkward moment means that you must speak or have the right answer. Having the awkward conversation well (calmly, without personalizing it, seeking to honor God and obey Scripture) is often more important to peacemaking than immediately resolving the issue. Rushing leads to foolishness and harshness. Pay attention to whether your offendedness is primarily asking for repentance toward yourself (which is eventually appropriate if you were sinned against) or toward God. Are you more concerned with your honor or receiving the attention that God deserves in this moment?

If I am more concerned about the other person's being right with God, then my hurts (and even the subsequent protective measures that may be biblically warranted) become much less reactive. For example, someone's coarse jokes do not define me and humiliate me; they embarrass me and reveal the speaker's need for God's work in his heart. I am hurt and desire the person to repent. I recognize, however, that until he realizes that his words reveal his heart (Luke 6:45) and are offensive to God, the person's repentance to me will be superficial and of little eternal value.

Personal Reflection: What aspects of the description of being a peacemaker challenge you most? What remaining questions do you have regarding how being a peacemaker equips you to be wisely vulnerable? What changes do you need to make in order to become more of a peacemaker?

What is the first thought that pops into your mind when conflict begins? What types of conflicts do you tend to personalize? How do you personalize them? How does personalizing conflict distract from the offender's primary dishonor of God and cause you to overly fear vulnerability?

Prayer: Lord, I would rather endure [detested activity] than endure conflict. I wish patience did not require an agitant, courage require fear, and peacemaking require conflict. But you tell me that facing conflict and aiding peace makes me your child (Matt. 5:9). In the moment, I do not see the payoff—only the pain. Trying to be a peacemaker aggravates two of my fears: rejection because of the hostility and failure if I cannot make peace happen. I forget that you call me only to be faithful, not effective. Faithfulness without effectiveness feels like failure, but I can see how that makes me like Jesus. He was faithful, was painfully rejected, seemingly failed, and yet brought great peace. This may be the hardest thing I have done, but I will try to stay engaged during conflict and keep my mind on you.

"THOSE WHO ARE PERSECUTED AND REVILED"

☐ Yes ☐ No ___ /10 Intensity ___ /8 Rank

Description: If mercy requires accepting unfairness, being persecuted and reviled means facing things that are attacking and untrue. With mercy, I voluntarily and sacrificially embrace unfairness. With being persecuted and reviled, it is forced upon me. With mercy, I have a choice. With being persecuted and reviled, that choice is taken away. Persecution and being reviled reveal who my enemies are. To be persecuted and reviled by the world means that I have identified with Christ and truth.

Benefit for Vulnerability: Other opposites of vulnerability are people-pleasing and naively believing that everyone can get along. Vulnerability must be willing to accept that there will be opposition. Too often an idealized view that people are basically good makes real vulnerability feel as though it should be irrelevant or easy. The logic says that if everyone realized their loving potential, we would not need to be vulnerable; we could just be perpetually affirmed for our uniqueness and individuality.

A willingness to face persecution and being reviled gives needed grit to vulnerability. It allows vulnerability to exist in a fallen world. When we expect to live without resistance, stress, or opposition (even in our close circle of relationships), the inevitable disappointment tempts us to retreat into a shell of self-protectiveness. But having a vulnerability that expects opposition is "blessed" because it is the only type of vulnerability that can be maintained.

Implementation: This is not a call to be quarrelsome. It is not a call to look for a fight. It is a call to prevent the inevitability of opposition from causing you to draw back from being lovingly real. How do you do this? Start with interactions that are relationally distant enough that you can patiently consider your response. Read books with which you disagree. Watch news programs that oppose or revile your political preference. These things allow you to practice engaging in the dialogue without becoming personal or defensive when the opposing person is not yet physically present.

Then move to "live" contexts by having meaningful conversations with people who have different views from your own. If they attack you or become defensive, seek a way to bless them. Compliment their vigor to get things right, even when you disagree with them on what right is. Never lose the clear conviction of being pure in heart, but recognize that a vulnerability that never enters hostile ground is not vulnerability with a biblical mission.

Personal Reflection: What aspects of the description of being persecuted and reviled challenge you most? What remaining questions do you have regarding how being persecuted and reviled equips you to be wisely vulnerable? What changes do you need to make in order to become more willing to be persecuted and reviled?

When have you been persecuted for your faith? How could you have made Christ's love more evident in that moment? How can you slow your thoughts and maintain a focus on what is most important in the midst of persecution?

Prayer: Lord, it saddens me to face persecution for your sake, because it means that people are attacking you in me. That is so backward, confused, hopeless, and blind (Matt. 6:23). I pray that you will help me to see that their despair is greater than my pain. I will need you in order to endure and not lose sight of my hope (1 Peter 2:20). There are so many distractions in the midst of persecution. My thoughts are tempted to turn to so many places other than to you. As I hear my name taken in vain by those who revile me because of you, prepare me to provide a response that answers their ultimate question, not just their temporal assault (Col. 4:6; 1 Peter 3:15).

WHAT DO I DO NOW?

Please do not put this booklet away and never look at it again. A single reading of a booklet that is primarily a guided personal reflection will not accomplish the purpose for which you began reading. Vulnerability (or the lack thereof) is a lifestyle, not an idea.

Write your reflections in a notebook or journal. Writing can make vulnerability easier. Once you have organized your thoughts and do not feel as though you are just rambling about unrelated issues, sharing should be less intimidating.

Identify a person with whom you can share these reflections: a trusted Christian friend, pastor, or counselor. The encouragement of others is important to any prolonged effort. Growing in vulnerability is no different. As was said earlier, choose wisely and persevere with these people.

Patiently commit to working on each area. This is not a race. Use this booklet to approach life as a relational and character-building scavenger hunt. Recognize that God usually works slowly in our lives over a period of time. Resist the urge to wish that God would just take this away. That will only breed unnecessary discouragement. Rather, thank God for his patience and grace that as you grow in vulnerability, you can still serve, worship, and enjoy him in the process.